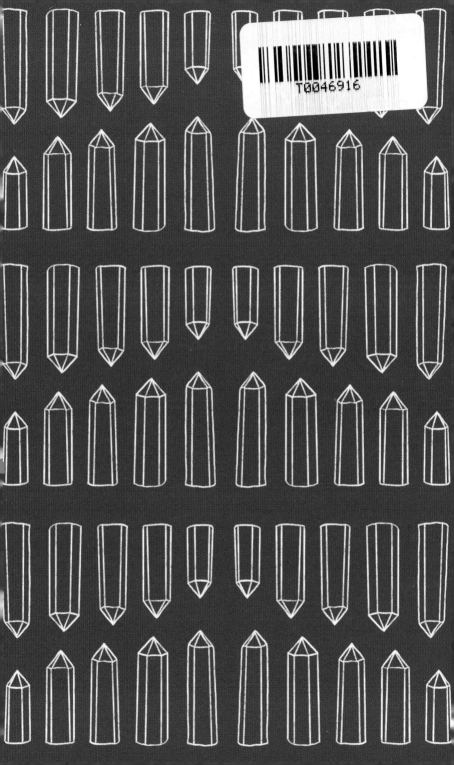

PRAISE FOR TRISTA MATEER

"*Artemis Made Me Do It* is a face-wetting collection that I wish I could read for the first time again. It's a reminder that you can't keep femininity in a cage, to hug the past versions of yourself, and to have hope for the pages you've yet to write."
— Michaela Angemeer, author of *You'll Come Back to Yourself*

"*Aphrodite Made Me Do It* is a dazzling portal of a collection. Trista Mateer erupts with spells of thunder and then gifts you with a careful platter of language to cast them yourself."
— Blythe Baird, author of *If My Body Could Speak*

"Trista Mateer's work has the kind of sumptuous quality that leaves you breathless. *Aphrodite Made Me Do It* is an incredible offering from a truly valuable poetic voice that channels love as the ancient and powerful emotion that it is. Combined with the poet's own art, this book is a vibrant labyrinth, a treat for every reader. Mateer is magnificent as always."
— Nikita Gill, author of *Fierce Fairytales*

Finalist - 2019 Goodreads Choice Awards — Poetry (*Aphrodite Made Me Do It*)

"Gut truths and gin-clear imagery, Trista Mateer reminds us of all those places left unexplored by language." (*Honeybee*)
— *Foreword Reviews*

"This is a collection that will beg you to be dog-eared, coffee-stained, and shared." (*Honeybee*)
— Amanda Lovelace, author of *the princess saves herself in this one*

ARTEMIS MADE ME DO IT

poems, prose, art

TRISTA MATEER

central
avenue
PUBLISHING

2022

Published by Central Avenue Publishing, an imprint of Central Avenue Marketing Ltd.
www.centralavenuepublishing.com

ARTEMIS MADE ME DO IT

978-1-77168-272-5 (pbk)
978-1-77168-273-2 (ebk)

Published in Canada

Printed in United States of America

1. POETRY / Women Authors   2. POETRY / Subject & Themes - General

10 9 8 7 6 5 4 3 2

For the lost girls.

*After all those years spent looking back,
may we move forward together.*

FOREWORD

My aunt once called me a feral child. I liked hearing it so much, I made her say it three times over, like it was a spell. When I think of words like feral, wild, and free . . . I think of Artemis.

Consider a goddess so free that even the most ancient patriarchal structure struggled to constrain her. Consider a goddess who stood defiant in a time when women were seen as wives and mothers and little else.

That is what Trista Mateer brings to life in *Artemis Made Me Do It*. Through verse that sings war songs as well as moon songs, the Artemis in these pages challenges and encourages. She lifts you out of despair and into fierceness. There are poems in here that will wound you and poems that will heal you, with an elegance that glows through every word.

But this isn't just a book of magnificent poetry.

This is the wildfire inside you that you have forgotten.

This is the wolf that sets you free.

— Nikita Gill
celebrated poet and
author of *Great Goddesses*

TRIGGERS

blood/gore
body image
death/grief
domestic abuse
emotional abuse
rape
sexual harassment

and possibly more

CONTENTS

ARTEMIS

Greek goddess of the hunt, the wild, the moon, young girls, archery,
and self-ownership. Daughter of Zeus and Leto. Twin sister of Apollo.
She is one of three maiden goddesses, "virginal" in the ancient sense:
beholden to no man, forever free to make her own decisions
and to tread her own path.

sacred to her (non-exhaustive list)
honeysuckle, cypress, amethyst, moss agate, deer, dogs, bears, bows
and arrows, mugwort, dreamwork, wilderness, marshes, and lakes.

NAMES TO KNOW

Apollo	god of light, archery, medicine, and prophecy, among others; twin brother of Artemis
Callisto	a nymph (minor nature goddess), daughter of King Lycaon of Arcadia, follower and favorite of Artemis
Diana	Roman goddess associated with Artemis
Dionysus	god of feasting, wine, fertility, and more
Hera	goddess of women, marriage, and childbirth; Queen of Olympus alongside Zeus
Leto	goddess of motherhood, mother of the twin gods Artemis and Apollo
Orion	a great hunter and companion of Artemis
Persephone	goddess of spring, nature, and death; Queen of the Underworld; half-sister and companion of Artemis
Zeus	god of sky and thunder, King of the Olympian gods, father of Artemis, Apollo, and others

lonely

dis connected

INTRODUCTION

Here I am
knowing the difference
between honey and the bee,

still chasing
what stings.

I don't know
what I want,
but I know
I need change.

What I mean is,
things rarely turn out
the way I expect them to.

What I mean is,
I've grown paranoid
and jumpy.

I cancel my dates.
I carry my keys between
my fingers

and I wonder how
deeply they could cut
into
a stranger.

BURNED OUT

I resent my own resiliency.
I don't want to bounce back.
I don't want to be strong.
Trample me underfoot
and just let me stay down.
God, just let me stay down.

more and
more

I find myself
exhausted by
everyday
living

THE URGE

to dream of moss and amethyst, to listen for the call of
the wild, to raise your siblings, to mother your friends,
to love with sharp teeth, to protect what is tender, to not
turn your head away from the blood, to run off and start
from nothing, to live slowly and deliberately, to chase
what needs chasing, to hope the deer makes it across
the road, to raise a hand against what does you harm, to
crawl back from the grave, to put faith in the stars, to
return to the forest of your youth, to wade through the
river of grief, to thank god for your own breath but then
take it back and thank only yourself

THE DREAM GOES LIKE THIS

I'm on the verge of sleep and then I'm not. I'm in the dark. I'm in the dark and it's too dark and I can't tell where I am, so I reach out a hand. I feel greenery, leaves, some kind of plant life. There's a howl in the distance. Then there's movement to my left and my body jolts into action. Fight or flight kicks in, and I am running for my life. I am stumbling in the pitch-darkness, tripping over roots, sick over the sound of my own heart beating so loudly that I am sure everything around me can hear my panic.

I lose my footing and crash through the trees, landing in an ungraceful heap in a clearing full of moonlight. I can see everything now. I am scuffed and muddy and bleeding from the lip, on my knees in front of my mother. And she takes my face in her palms and she says, "This isn't right." And I'm crying because of course she's correct. This isn't right. Nothing is right.

And then she's not my mother anymore, because she's the moon. No, she's something else. Something old and dangerous. Fear returns to me as she pins me in place with her gaze.

"You've forgotten
how to feed the beast
inside of you," she says,

"and it's hungry."

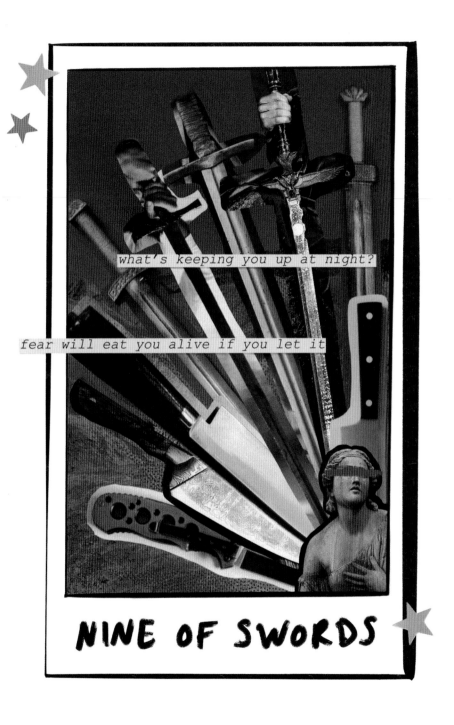

what's keeping you up at night?

fear will eat you alive if you let it

NINE OF SWORDS

ARTEMIS AIRS HER GRIEVANCES

I have the same complaints
as most women before me.

I have been romanticized,
mythologized,
separated from myself
and then pieced back together
so many times
no one remembers
the truth of who I am.

There are so many versions of me.
Not even I recognize all of my faces.

They say Mother, though I bore no children. They say Virgin, though I lie with women. They say Protectress, though death follows me. They threw Selene aside and called me Moon Goddess. They drowned Britomartis and called me Lady of the Lake. I am inextricable from the women who came before me. I am half woman, half myth of myself. This is what happens when you sit back and allow other people to dictate who you are. I will never bite my tongue like that again.

I AM THE GOLDEN ARROW.
I AM ANGER CAUGHT IN THE THROAT.
I AM WHAT PROWLS THE WOODS AT NIGHT.
I AM WHAT WANTS AND DEVOURS.
I AM THE HEART ON FIRE.

Time is a strange thing.
They say I was born

and then immediately tasked with
helping to deliver my brother Apollo.

I supposed eldest daughters
never really get to be children for long.

Domestic life became a burden to me
before it ever had a chance

to be anything else.

there was
so much
responsibility
on my shoulders

so
young

too
much

As I grew I saw my brother raised high, always the golden child. Apollo with his light-bringing. Apollo with his bow and arrows. Apollo with his freedom. It wasn't an angry kind of envy, but it was envy nonetheless. I saw what he had, what he was given, the life he was allowed to lead.

And I wanted it for myself.

When I told my mother what I desired,
she held me close to her chest and said,
"I remember what it was like
to want more than this."

She was quiet for so long afterward.

Fiercely determined
to be the architect of my own fate,
I went to the mountain-home of my father
and I petitioned Zeus.

I did not hold back the truth of it.
I told him who I was.

A LIST OF ~~REQUESTS~~ DEMANDS

I want as many names and titles as my brother.
I want to be as known as he is in the world.
I want to have a bow and quiver like his.
I want to be known as a bringer of light.

I will not be sitting around and weaving;
I will have my feet in the earth
and blood on my hands.
I will wear a dress I can hunt in.

And I will have a place to call my own,
not a town or a city.
I want all the forests of the world.
The dark, deep places.

Always, I will be surrounded
by a band of beautiful nymphs.

I will never be beholden to a man.
I will answer only to myself.
And I will never marry.

Like most fathers,
he misunderstood me.

And like most daughters,
I never bothered to correct him.

I took his acceptance and ran with it.

●oooo Olympus LTE 11:54 PM 7%
Messages
zeus
More...
i love girls
That's nice, honey.
i never want to marry a man
You don't have to.
You can remain a virgin forever!
?????

You no longer know what you want because you have spent years prioritizing the needs of others. They told you, *This is what Woman does.*

Woman minimizes her suffering. Woman stays where she's useful. Woman gives up her body. Woman gives up her time. Woman sacrifices herself on the altar of bad love. Woman pours until she is empty. Woman gives until there is nothing left of her. Woman disappears day by day and there are no search parties and there are no dogs. No one even knows she is missing.

When I need to remember
who I am and what I stand for,

I do what all women
must eventually do:

I go out
into life's wilderness
to find myself.

are you wallowing in familiar despair

instead of moving forward

five of cups

THE POET AIRS HER GRIEVANCES

What if everyone feels as lonely as I do? What if this is just what life is like? What if nobody really gets what they want? What if I worry myself to death? What if I was on WebMD this morning and I definitely am worrying myself to death? What if I'm not cut out for this? What if I've waited too long to change? What if I'm sick of the stagnancy but still can't get out of bed? What if I'm not good, like other people are good? What if poetry is the only place I feel comfortable being honest? What if I rarely recognize my own face? What if I have second thoughts every time I walk out the front door? What if I don't want to talk about grief even though I'm always choking on it? What if I don't know how to carry this alone? What if I never really know myself well? What if my entire personality is made of trauma responses and coping mechanisms? What if I'm too tired to try to get better? What if I can't ever afford therapy? What if I'm broken? What if I never get closure? What if I never move on? What if I only look forward to sleeping and never to being awake? What if it always feels safer to be alone? What if I always have to act okay but I never actually get to be okay again? What if life is unbearable forever and not just for now?

POEM IN WHICH HAVING A YOUNGER BROTHER IS COMPLICATED

It's hard to watch him
make the same mistakes
I curse other men for

and still
want to defend him.

There was a time
when I treated red flags
like roses,

happy to be handed anything.

MY MOTHER MARRIED A MAN WHO YELLS

in this way, he is like and unlike my father.

a man who would scream
at a can of tuna he can't get open
versus
a man who would raise his voice
at anything to unnerve it.

one
I watched yell
at my brother
until the boy pissed himself.

one
I watched yell
at a chair
he stubbed his toe on.

both times I felt like I couldn't breathe.

truth is, the man doesn't matter anymore.

just the timbre.
just the volume.
just the anger.

It is not my father's fault that I continue
to run away from good love, but

he is the reason I know it is an option.

It is not my mother's fault that I continue
to chase people who make me feel small
and unsure of myself,

but she is the reason I grew up thinking
that's what love looked like.

After a while you start to wonder,
am I the thing that is wrong?

Am I unlovable?

Am I unwantable?

Am I really this easy to hurt?

Am I really this easy to leave?

My mother would rather be miserable than alone.
She asks me to run errands with her just to have

someone to fight with. She tells me that pickiness
leads to loneliness and that I don't want to get to

her age and be alone. She says I don't want to get
to her age and have no one. She says, "Read less."

She says, "Go outside." She pulls the lipstick from
her purse and holds it up to my face. She says,

"This isn't your color, but it should work fine."
She says, "That's all anyone can really ask for."

and now everyone says

*WHEN ARE YOU GOING
TO GET MARRIED*

*WHEN ARE YOU GOING
TO HAVE CHILDREN*

*WHEN ARE YOU GOING
TO SETTLE DOWN*

what if

I don't realize

I'm killing my soul

until it's already happening

What if it

already

happened

sinking further into myself / becoming small / Russian doll creature / onion climbing back inside her layers / he put his hands on me and I turned docile / lost touch with my friends / locked up my shoes and coat / he plied me with tea and honey / and I grew too lazy to lift a hand in defense of myself / I didn't forget my own name but I forgot other things / watched the sun come up / chugged NyQuil before crawling into bed next to him / called it a sleeping potion / over-the-counter magic / his breath in the bed made me nervous until it didn't / I never really shook the nerves / just the urgency / got complacent and called it love / let my body wither under my own care / I put curlers in while he was at work / I made small talk with his mother / watched the way she moved through the house / and ghosted after her / specter in a nightgown washing dishes / baking pies / contemplating death at the kitchen table / I thought domesticity was an illness until I realized I was sick on bad love / by the time I left I was clawing out of my own skin / aching for a moment of beauty that had nothing to do with my body

Upstairs, the gentle sobbing of my mother, the heaving of her chest because I'm not beautiful like she wanted me to be. I take her hand, palm up, and make her feel the hair on my face until she yanks herself away.

She called it disgusting once, but now she just says nothing. She buys me shapewear and Dolce & Gabbana perfume and three different kinds of depilatory creams that smell like chemicals and leave my face red but not smooth. I keep taking her hand, palm up, to remind her that it's there. I wax it and it grows back—like me, so stubborn under all that makeup.

I pull on Spanx and think of death and when I'm done thinking of death, I think of God, and when I'm done thinking of God, I fall backwards onto my bed and try to feel small. It isn't hard.

I think of my mother upstairs.

it's getting harder to believe the natural state of my body is inherently wrong

"Do you still write about me?" they ask,

but I have never stopped writing about anyone.

I write poems for you
the way other people
bring flowers to graves.

i used to wonder how the mermaid
could give up her voice
for a chance at love,

but i'm starting to understand it.

sometimes i think i'd put down the pen
if it would make things less complicated.
if it would give me an easier life.

i could be small and quiet.

i could do that.

be bold

you will overcome

Queen of Wands

ARTEMIS LAMENTS

Look at you,

taking care of everyone but yourself,
letting love make you hollow
instead of full.

They say even Aphrodite has no power over my heart.
That wasn't always as true as it is now.

Faithful companion to the end,
I put Orion's body in the sky when he died.

I've stood over the graves of
warriors, hunters, and friends.

Love wounds us in so many different ways.

but Callisto

was the hardest to lose

favorite of mine,

dearest in all my heart

Some say Zeus did it to protect her.
As if he could protect
what he himself had made unsafe,
what he himself had broken.

Some say Hera did it out of jealousy,
but it wasn't her.

It was me.

I turned Callisto into a bear
after my father disguised himself as me
to lure her close
and rape her.

She had no idea who she was after that.
No idea what had been done to her.

In my grief and anger,
I thought it a kindness.

Better, this way.
Better to be able to outrun.
Better to be able to bite back.
Better to be monstrous
than touched by monsters.
Let her curse my name.
Let her forget her own.
Let her forget.
Just let her forget.

MISSTEP AFTER MISSTEP

What is fifteen years to an immortal?
Nothing. And everything.

I replayed the day over in my head on a loop. I could have
done a thousand other things, but none of them would
have made her safer. You cannot hide a girl from a god-
king. Zeus had eyes everywhere and Hera's reputation
for punishment was more well-known than even mine.
It didn't matter if Zeus was the aggressor. Haven't you
heard the stories? My own mother was chased from
Olympus after he had his way with her.

At least among the trees, Callisto had a chance to be free.
Bears are sacred to me, as she was sacred to me. I knew
it wasn't enough, but the Fates intervened before I had
another chance to.

Sometime after her assault, Callisto gave birth to a
human son. Arcas. I scooped up the babe and sent him
to live in the city. There was no need for their paths to
ever cross again, and yet, they did.

During those fifteen years, Arcas grew into a mighty
hunter himself. (Of course he would, just like his
mother.) In the woods with his bow, he happened upon
Callisto trapped in bear form. And he hunted her. (Of
course he would, just like his father.)

She could not be left alone
to live unhindered.

Someone was always
going to be after her.

I turned Callisto
into a constellation
when she was killed.

Ursa Major

my big bear

OUR LOVE IS SO SMALL NOW
BARELY A SPARK

I CAN'T SEE IT AT ALL NOW
EXCEPT IN THE DARK

You must
be in touch
with your rage
and your anger
and your darkness.

When I thought I was lost,
I used those feelings
to propel me forward.

Those dreams we had when the world was younger, I hope they can still come true.

Remember there is more to life than trauma and ruin. Even when it doesn't feel like it. Grief makes you feel small, though you are not small. Grief makes you feel weak, though you are not weak.

On nights when my heart is heaviest, Apollo brings the poetry and Dionysus brings the wine. Persephone sets out the fruit and honey cakes. We feast with the Muses and the Graces. Everyone dances until dawn. Their laughter lifts me and their voices sing me home.

The question is not
whether you will be hurt
by this life.

You will be hurt.

The question is:
What will you do
in the aftermath?

Will you swallow grief
or will grief swallow you?

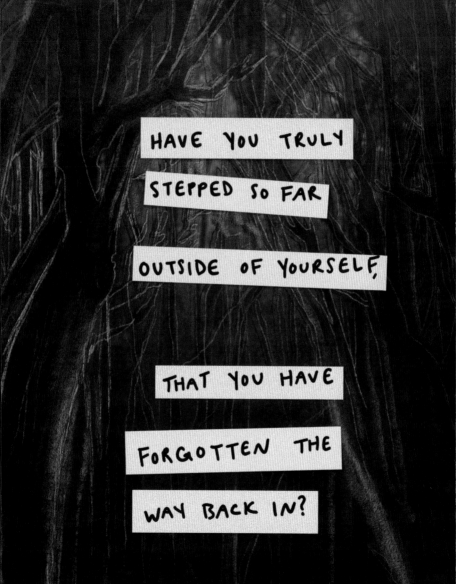

HAVE YOU TRULY
STEPPED SO FAR
OUTSIDE OF YOURSELF,
THAT YOU HAVE
FORGOTTEN THE
WAY BACK IN?

It is time to come back.
I am calling you home
to the forest of yourself.

subconscious
fear

anxiety

uncertainty

THE MOON

THE POET LAMENTS

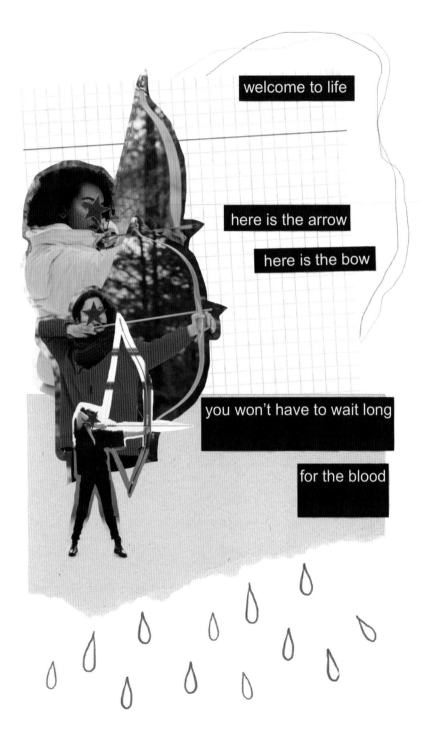

welcome to life

here is the arrow

here is the bow

you won't have to wait long

for the blood

Not too loud, girl. Keep your head down, girl. Stay safe, girl. They only want one thing, girl. You better not give it to them, girl. Keep your legs shut, girl. Keep your mouth shut, girl. Why so timid, girl? You're so boring, girl. Such a tease, girl. Don't be basic, girl. Don't be like other girls, girl. Learn your cues, girl. Laugh on command, girl. Smile, girl. What did you think would happen, girl? What were you wearing, girl? Learn faster, girl. Keep up, girl. Forgive and forget, girl. Accidents happen, girl. Take the blame, girl. Try less makeup, girl. Cover up, girl. You're too forward, girl. You're asking for it, girl. Why don't you dance, girl? Why don't you leave the house, girl? Lose some weight, girl. Fix your face, girl. Beauty is pain, girl. Anticipate needs, girl. Sacrifice, girl. Don't stand out, girl. Don't fit in, girl. Please everyone but yourself, girl. Grin and bear it, girl. I told you to smile, girl. Don't be rude, girl. Don't be needy, girl. Don't want too much, girl. Don't eat too much, girl. How'd you get so thin, girl? How'd you get so quiet?

And I believe all men think of me as a person.
Correction: *not all men.*

And I believe all men care about consent.
Correction: *not all men.*

And I believe all men walking behind me at night
Correction: *not all men.*

are going to keep their distance,
Correction: *not all men.*

or they are going to pass me by
Correction: *not all men.*

without a second thought
Correction: *not all men.*

about my body
Correction: *not all men.*

and what could be done to it
Correction: *not all men.*

so quickly
Correction: *not all men.*

in the dark.

The wolf caught me in his jaws
but when I cried out,
others only said:

I have seen the wolf many times
and he has not bitten me.

Spent nineteen years of my life learning pretty. Learning sacrifice. Learning the practice of everyday pain. I used all the right words. I bought the lingerie. I laughed on command like a child's doll with a pull string. I preened. I nested. I let them put their hands wherever they wanted to put their hands. I was polite enough not to resist it.

I was   polite enough not to resist it.

I did say no ~~when he~~

~~when I~~

I yelled when I thought he couldn't hear me.
I don't know why I thought he couldn't hear me.

I wanted him to not have heard me.
I needed it.
What an easy solution.
What a forgivable trespassing. But

nobody cared what I wanted.

Forgive me if I unlearn pretty
and learn vicious
in its place.

IT'S NOT RIGHT
THAT I WILL
CARRY THE WEIGHT
OF THIS NIGHT
FOREVER

AND YOU CAN
WALK AWAY LIKE
NOTHING HAPPENED

unnatural disaster

Survivors are often angry.
Angry at the disaster. Angry at
god. Angry at being called one
of the lucky ones. Angry at fate.
Angry at themselves. Angry at
everyone else. The anger is not
the problem. The earthquake is
the problem. The wildfire.

The hurricane. The sinkhole.

The man and his unwanted hands.

He thought I belonged to him.

I thought I did too, for a while.

ON BEING STALKED

Roses smashed on the front porch. Bobby pins mailed back one by one. A shadow is just a shadow until it starts to scare you. A man is just a man until he reaches for your throat. Until he watches you from parked cars and street corners. Slashes your tires. Shows up at your job. Follows you out of town. So yes,

YES.

I set aside my quiet.
I bought a pocketknife.
I shrieked at him on the street.
I caused a scene at every
public place he showed up.

People called it unladylike, said he was just acting out of love, said men were animals but I was *crazy*. Maybe they were right, but I felt powerless until the day I realized that hell is a place other people put you, and I could put us

both

there.

Once upon a time,
I saw a boy
who looked like my rapist,

and my entire body
forgot how to work.

I CAN'T TELL THE DIFFERENCE
BETWEEN A MAN WHO ISN'T
DANGEROUS AND A MAN WHO
HAS SIMPLY LEARNED TO
BEHAVE AS IF HE IS NOT
DANGEROUS. I TREAT EVERY
ONE LIKE A SNAKE IN TALL
GRASS. COULD BE HARMLESS.
COULD COST ME MY LIFE.

—I DON'T WANT TO, I HAVE TO

CRAZY MAN-HATING FEMINIST BITCH

small attacks. all the time. and then you learn it's war?
and you're not supposed to name the enemy?

men are not my enemy in this story,
but they have been and they probably will be again.

I SIT ON THE COUCH WITH MY MOTHER WHILE WE WATCH YOU ON NETFLIX

I sit on the couch with my mother while we watch a man do another unspeakable thing to a woman for fun. What I mean is, he does it for fun and we watch it for fun. What I mean is, I am watching my mother watch Penn Badgley wash blood off of his hands, and I am waiting to see how quickly she forgives him—the same way she forgave the hands around my neck, the tires removed from my car, the screaming in my workplace.

I sit on the couch with my mother while she watches TV and I think about the time she called my stalker a romantic. She said he just loved me. He just loved me so much.   He just loved me so much he waited in parking lots at night to see who I'd go home with. He just loved me so much he trailed me out of the city at 2 p.m. on a Tuesday, lost his job because he couldn't stop following me around, started mailing me his sweaters and threatening suicide and—

I sit on the couch with my mother while we watch the credits hit the screen and she turns to me and says, "Love was never going to be enough for him."

And I say, "I know."

grief pours into me

and rage pours out

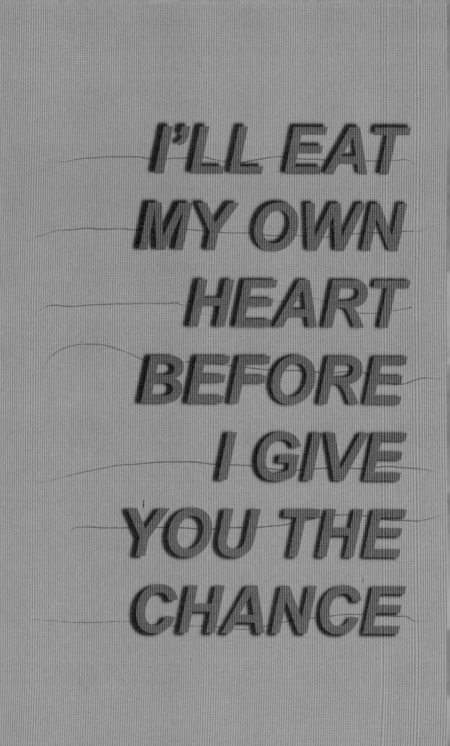

You called me a girl,
but I am a portrait
of the world on fire.
You called me a girl,
but I am a bruise
that refuses to heal.
You called me a girl,
but I am a knife.

DEER/DEAR

I always hope
she makes it across the road

and when she makes it across the road,
I always hope
the other side is safer.

I hope she lives to meet
her sister's children.
I hope she gets a mouthful
of blackberry.

I hope for a moment at least,
life gets to be sweet for her.
That it gets to be easy.

I always wonder
if she knows
both of us
have been prey.

follow your
instincts

the high priestess

ARTEMIS SPEAKS ON THE HUNT

girlhood
itself

is a thing
you *must*

be brave
to endure

You have been taught
to hush the voice inside of you

when it calls for rest
when it calls for better
when it calls for justice
when it calls for more

and the less you listen to it,
the quieter it gets.

After our long hunts across the mountains, the nymphs and I would retire to a secret grove deep in the forest. We used to laze about naked in the hot spring, enjoying each other's company, kissing and laughing and singing.

But women are never allowed safety for long. There is always another grasping hand. Another hungry mouth. Another prying eye.

Actaeon, out with his dogs, was not the first man to hunt me.

when you
say you want
nothing to do
with a man,
must it
always be

taken as a
challenge

???

EVEN WHEN IT'S NOT, I BRACE FOR
THE IMPACT REGARDLESS. SURVIVAL
DEMANDS IT. I KNOW WHAT HAPPENS
TO GIRLS WHO SAY **NO** WITHOUT
COATING IT IN SUGAR FIRST.

First, he took to the hunting grounds, singing his own praises. He boasted loud enough for anyone to hear that he was a better hunter than me, that it was he who should be lord of the forest.

I refused him the attention.

He went second to my temple, declaring his intention to marry me. To stake his claim. "Come in from the wilds, beauty. Stoke the fires in my house. Mother my children. Set down your bow."

I gave no response to the arrogant fool.

Dissatisfied with my disinterest,
he did what so many men have done.

He decided to subdue.
He decided to muzzle.
He decided to take.

When Actaeon found me bathing in the hot spring, he hid himself amongst the trees and let his eyes wander. He let his hands wander too. He ████████████████ █████████████████████

For a moment,
everything was a blur of motion.
Water splashing.
Women shrieking.

In the end
I refused him
even the kindness
of a quick death.

I turned him into a stag
with a flick of my wrist
and a splash of springwater.

Then I sent his dogs after him.

They said, "If you keep carrying
on like this, you won't even be the
person people root for in your own
stories."

I said, "Good."

YOU WILL
RESPECT ME
OR YOU WILL
FEAR ME
ENOUGH TO
LEAVE ME
ALONE

I have a brutal history with men.
I won't shy away from that.

Every woman
eventually
has a brutal history
with men.

I have no qualms about spilling blood.
I will always be my fiercest advocate,
my defender,
my protector.

I'd rather they call me cruel
than catch me.

When they romanticize your wild,
be wary.

Too often
they see you as something to be tamed.
New puppy, not wolf.
Something to show off.
Sharp tongue on a leash.
Claws clipped neatly.
Feral creature whittled down
to almost nothing.

Too often
it makes them feel powerful
to grab something unbroken
and hold it
by the throat.

*IT IS NOT
IN YOUR NATURE
TO BE DOCILE.*

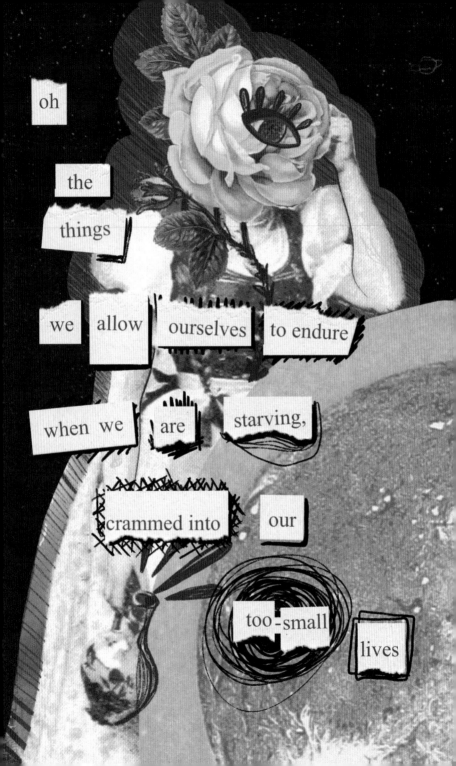

oh

the

things

we allow ourselves to endure

when we are starving,

crammed into our

too-small lives

You are wolf.
You are witch.
You are goddess.
You are moon.
You are mountain.
You are wound.
You are weapon.
You are creature.
You are beast.
You are sea.
You are darkness.
You are sun.
You are fire.
You are star.
You are magick.
You are myth.
You are famine.
You are feast.
You are free.
Don't you see?

Normalizing the things
that kill your spirit

is a slow but sure path
toward decay.

It erodes you
as the river does
to the cliff face.
It steals you,
piece

by
piece.

wholeness and completion

reflect on how far you have come

everything is coming full circle

the world

THE POET EMBRACES THE CHASE

YOU

DESERVE

THE WORLD

When did I learn to lie down and roll over? To play doormat? To be grateful if men wiped their feet on me instead of laying a hand on me? To say please and thank you afterwards? To let my girlhood be defined by fear and then to let my womanhood follow in its footsteps?

I'm in love with my anger / my
war-won body / tense and vicious.

SHE OF THE WOODS

Swamp creature. All unwashed mouth, all river mud. You overgrown bramble. You outrageous thorn. Unafraid of a little blood. Unafraid of a lot. Opposition trembles before you. Runs away and tells stories of your unholiness. Your dirt and your anger. All your bite. Reputation doesn't precede you; it follows you around with its tail between its legs. It cowers in your shadow. Curse the words of those who tried to bury you. Bless your inability to stay down.

I don't know why
I keep their names
out of my poetry.
They don't deserve it.

I KEEP THEIR NAMES
OUT OF MY POETRY
BECAUSE I MUST
ALLOW MYSELF
A SAFE PLACE.
I DESERVE THAT.

He says he loves feminine women.

Not too much makeup though.
Sexy but not too sexy, you know?
Not funny, but she laughs at everything.
Comes when she's called but doesn't call too often.
Not too bitchy.
Submissive. Subservient.

I tell him he has mistaken
obedience for femininity.

I suggest getting a dog instead

but I caution that both bitches bite back.

I refuse to make myself small enough
to fit inside the cramped box
of your desire.

I thought for years that if I wasn't orbiting around Venus, I'd be drifting aimlessly through my life without a purpose. Never stopped to wonder why I felt like I needed a purpose. Never stopped to wonder why I thought romantic love was the greatest thing I could do with my life. Never stopped to wonder why my life needed to be great and couldn't just be lived.

I have been many different versions of myself.
I regret that I have not known all of them well.
I regret that I have not treated all of them well.

do you weep when your inner child weeps?

do you even know what you have lost?

FOR MY BROTHER

I miss you even when you're just leaving the room / we spent years growing up in the same one / I glow inside when I see you happy / I wish I had all of my adventures with you / I wish I was in every single one of your stories / I hope I die before you so I never again have to live in a world without you in it / the first few years of my life must have been so empty / I will never grow out of wanting to protect you / you will always be small to me even though you are big now / leaving home was the hardest thing I ever had to do because you were in it / you're the reason all of my favorite things are my favorite things.

*EVERY DAY
I AM FALLING
BACK IN LOVE
WITH PIECES
OF MYSELF.*

Under the light
of the full moon

I release myself from fear

and I release myself

from worry

EASY WAYS OF EXPLORING YOUR INTERNAL WILDERNESS

- regular routine journaling
- keeping an art, tarot, or dream journal
- creating something / self-expression
- dancing
- meditating
- keeping houseplants / tending a garden
- collecting things you're drawn to
- writing letters to friends
- setting boundaries
- starting a bucket list
- not monetizing your hobbies
- dream/vision boarding
- scripting/manifesting
- honoring your curiosity

JOURNAL PROMPTS

- write a letter to your younger self.
- write a letter to the person you are now.
- write a letter to your future self.
- what makes you feel most like yourself?
- what do you need to let go of?
- what do you need to forgive yourself for?
- what do you wish people knew about you?
- what are you avoiding thinking about? why?
- how would your life change if you didn't care what other people thought of your choices?

I'M DONE BEING
SAD ABOUT YOU IN
A BIG WAY BUT
I'M STILL NOT DONE
BEING SAD ABOUT
YOU IN SMALL
WAYS YET
OKAY?

IT DOESN'T HURT
TO MISS YOU
ANYMORE

I WELCOME
THE MEMORY OF YOU
WITH OPEN ARMS

THE TIME WE SHARED
TOGETHER WAS IMPORTANT
BUT NOW IT IS OVER

THAT DOESN'T HAVE
TO MEAN
FORGETTING

I MAKE SPACE FOR
MY FEELINGS BUT THEN
I MOVE ON

HOW LONG HAVE I BEEN DEDICATED TO MY OWN SELF-DESTRUCTION?

Time is rushing by faster every day.
Nothing on this rock makes any goddamn sense.

I am freshly committed to chasing what soothes me.
I desire only sweetness from now on.

I REFUSE TO BE A VICTIM OF STAGNANCY AGAIN

What did you do today?
Existed quietly within myself.
What will you do tomorrow?
Exist with some degree of force.

rain helps the
flowers grow

balance

patience

temperance

ARTEMIS: RESTORING

Rise again from death, shapeshifter.

Reroll the dice of your life. Remake the world in your image. Outrun the wolves at your door. Manifest a future where you never have to die again, but know that you could if you had to. You have fallen many times before.

DIANA

We run the same trails.
We endure the same trials.
Wear my name, as I wear yours.
I will not call you threat.
I will call you mirror.

Forgive yourself for the wounds you inflicted while you were hurting. Forgive yourself for standing on the edge of that cliff. Forgive yourself for the arrows and the blades and the blood and the sharpness of your own tongue. Forgive yourself for the damage you caused before you had words for your pain. Forgive yourself for standing in your own way. Forgive yourself for treating your sisters as enemies, for competing with your friends, for not seeing the bigger picture. Forgive yourself for seeing the bigger picture and ignoring it, choosing temporary safety over long-term happiness. Forgive yourself for the years you refused to raise a hand in defense of yourself, the years you suffered your own mistreatment.

IT IS TIME.

Your anger
is a divine instrument
for change.

But anger alone won't sustain you.
It won't even keep you warm.

TAKE A DEEP BREATH

May you brave your own wilderness.
May you finally face yourself
and accept what you see.
May you have the courage
to defend and rebuild.
May you find peace.

MAY PEACE
NEVER LULL YOU
INTO COMPLACENCY
AND INACTION

If you sit back
and wait patiently
for change,
it will not come in this lifetime.

Or the one after. Or the one after.
Or the one after. Or the one after.
Or the one after. Or the one after.
Or the one after. Or the one after.
Or the one after. Or the one after.
Or the one after. Or the one after.
Or the one after. Or the one after.
Or the one after. Or the one after.
Or the one after. Or the one after.
Or the one after. Or the one after.
Or the one after. Or the one after.
Or the one after. Or the one after.
Or the one after. Or the one after.
Or the one after. Or the one after.
Or the one after. Or the one after.
Or the one after. Or the one after.
Or the one after. Or the one after.
Or the one after. Or the one after.
Or the one after. Or the one after.
Or the one after. Or the one after.
Or the one after. Or the one after.
Or the one after. Or the one after.
Or the one after. Or the one after.
Or the one after. Or the

Teach your daughters to say no. Teach your daughters to raise their voices. Teach your daughters to make waves. To value safety over politeness. To yell *fire* instead of *help*. Teach your daughters to feel comfortable in their own bodies. Teach your daughters to live without shame. Teach your daughters to hit first. To bite back. To burn the world down when they are mistreated. Teach your daughters to out their abusers. To be deadly serious. To be dangerous. To be sure. To know what they want. Teach your daughters to take a stand. To be bold. To be brave. Teach your daughters to believe in a better world.

And then tell them they deserve one.

Say, *you do not have to suffer*
like I have suffered.

Say, *the legacy of girlhood*
does not have to be one of pain.

It hurts to rip open wounds
and reset bones.

It hurts to dig around inside
and see what's going on.

It hurts to realize how deeply
you have betrayed yourself over the years.

Healing will never be convenient.

You're going to be strange forever, girl.
Bursting at the seams of life.
Insatiable.
Snapping and howling.
Found and lost again.
Chasing dreams.
Making change.
Curious and mystifying.
Refusing to settle.
Refusing to slow down.
Lusting after joy.
Driving all night.
Cursing too much.
Laughing too loudly.
Back-talking.
Asking the moon for advice.
Swallowing the stars.
Rewriting your fate.
Holding your own hand.
Saying your own name.

HOW TO FEED YOUR WILD SOUL

Find your way,
again and again,
to what you love.

Life can still be beautiful
despite what you have seen,
despite what you have endured,
despite the years lost to loneliness
and mental illness
and trauma.

you're here.

you made it.

today you're on the other side

of something,

even if it's just a page.

You dream of safety, of peace, of paradise.

You want to fit into the world,
but it refuses to make a place for you.

Fine.

Make your own place.

Make a place for your soul to let its guard down. Leave behind what does not sustain you. Leave behind what does not coax joy right up to the surface of your life. Allow yourself room to relax. Let the animal of your body crawl out of its cave and stretch. Lean into the natural cycles of your life. Death and renewal. Winter and spring. Work toward what you love, then rest. Go out into the world, and then return to yourself. Always return to yourself.

solitude
is as
essential
as community

There is a calm center
inside of you
untouched
by the rest of the world.

You can return to this place
whenever you need to.

There is no easy way forward
that is worth taking.

The journey ahead is perilous
but it is bursting with sweetness
and meaning.

A gloriously brilliant
and surprising life
lies before you,

just off the beaten path.

TO BE CONTINUED...

YOU THINK HE HANDED ME A CROWN? I WAS QUEEN OF DEATH BEFORE THE GREEK PANTHEON EVEN EXISTED.

ACKNOWLEDGMENTS

Thank you so much to everyone who championed the first book, *Aphrodite Made Me Do It*, which made this book and series a possibility. I wouldn't be able to do what I love without the constant support of my readers, the poetry community, and BookTok!

Thank you to Michelle and the team at Central Avenue, everyone over at IPG, Lauren Zaknoun for her work on the cover, Jessica Peirce for her indispensable edits, Michaela Angemeer for offering such a lovely blurb, and Nikita Gill for her foreword as well as her constant support and guidance.

And last but definitely not least, my absolute gratitude to my early readers: Morgan Boyd, Michael Freitas, Catarine Hancock, Molly Ringle, and Caitlyn Siehl.

CREDITS

creative direction: Trista Mateer

editing: Jessica Peirce

proofreading: Molly Winter

photography: pexels

cover design: Lauren Zaknoun

interior illustrations: Trista Mateer

interior design: Michelle Halket

publisher: Central Avenue Publishing

sales & distribution: IPG

foreign & audio rights: Linda Migalti,
Susan Schulman Literary Agency

Trista Mateer is the award-winning and bestselling author of multiple poetry collections including *Aphrodite Made Me Do It* and *Honeybee*. She is a passionate mental health advocate, currently writing in South Carolina.

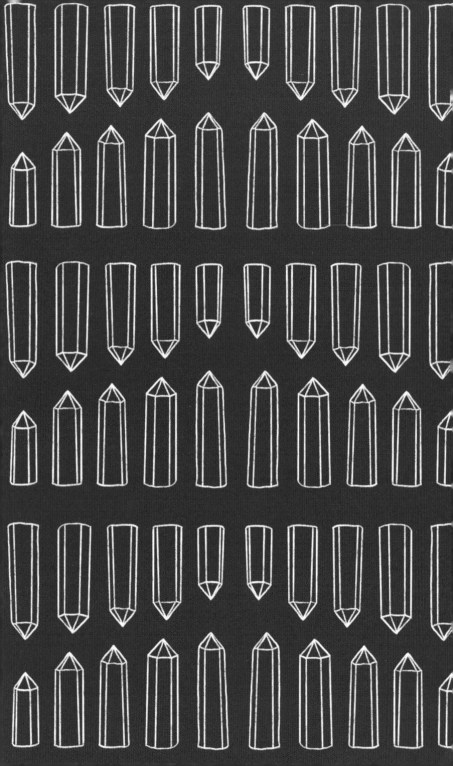